AMONG MEN

also by david yee

acquiesce
carried away on the crest of a wave
lady in the red dress
paper SERIES

AMONG MEN
david yee

PLAYWRIGHTS CANADA PRESS
toronto

among men © Copyright 2023 by David Yee
First edition: May 2023
Printed and bound in Canada by Imprimerie Gauvin, Gatineau

Jacket art and design Leon Aureus
Author photo © Dahlia Katz

Playwrights Canada Press
202-269 Richmond St. w., Toronto, ON M5V 1X1
416.703.0013 | info@playwrightscanada.com | www.playwrightscanada.com

LIBRARY AND ARCHIVES CANADA CATALOGUING IN PUBLICATION
Title: Among men / David Yee.
Names: Yee, David, 1977- author.
Description: First edition. | A play. .
Identifiers: Canadiana (print) 20230184103 | Canadiana (ebook) 20230184111
   | ISBN 9780369104373 (softcover) | ISBN 9780369104397 (EPUB)
   | ISBN 9780369104380 (PDF)
Classification: LCC PS8647.E44 A76 2023 | DDC C812/.6—dc23

Playwrights Canada Press operates on land which is the ancestral home of the Anishinaabe Nations (Ojibwe / Chippewa, Odawa, Potawatomi, Algonquin, Saulteaux, Nipissing, and Mississauga), the Wendat, and the members of the Haudenosaunee Confederacy (Mohawk, Oneida, Onondaga, Cayuga, Seneca, and Tuscarora), as well as Metis and Inuit peoples. It always was and always will be Indigenous land.

We acknowledge the financial support of the Canada Council for the Arts, the Ontario Arts Council (OAC), Ontario Creates, and the Government of Canada for our publishing activities.

For my mother,
who did her best to raise a good man.

For two months we quarrelled over socialism   poetry   how to
    boil water
doing the dishes   carpentry   Russian steel production figures
    and whether
you could believe them and whether Toronto Leafs would take it all
that year and maybe hockey was rather like a good jazz combo
never knowing what came next
Listening
how the new house built with salvaged old lumber
bent a little in the wind and dreamt of the trees it came from
    —AL PURDY, "HOUSE GUEST"

        my friend Al, union builder and cynic,
        hesitating to believe his own delicate poems
        lest he believe in something better than himself:
        and history, which is yet to begin,
        will exceed this, exalt this
        as a poem erases and rewrites its poet.
            —MILTON ACORN, "KNOWING I LIVE IN A DARK AGE"

                Storm clouds are gathering
                the wind is gonna blow,
                the race of man is suffering
                and I can hear the moan,
                'cause nobody,
                but nobody
                can make it out here alone.
                    —MAYA ANGELOU, "ALONE"

foreword

by Howard White

This gem of a play is the kind of drama I like best: comedy with heart. The two characters (there are only two) are highly unusual: boozy Canadian hosers on one hand and world-class verbal acrobats on another. Each is unforgettable in his own way. They are unlike in that one is well launched into a forty-year marriage and building his forever home, while the other is adrift in life and heartsick over a seemingly impossible love. They are alike in that they are both stalled in their greater passion: the desire to make it as writers. Both men live through language, which makes them highly entertaining subjects for the stage.

It is something of a distraction that the two characters and the setting are borrowed from real life. *among men* reimagines a few days in the late 1950s when the real Canadian poet, Al Purdy (1918–2000), and another real Canadian poet, Milton Acorn (1923–1986), are half-heartedly building Purdy's real A-frame cottage in Ameliasburgh, Ontario, imbibing Purdy's wild grape wine, and arguing over everything under the sun. I say a distraction because playwright David Yee does such a convincing job of recreating the speech mannerisms and personalities of these two legendary Canadian writers that the play has the real-life freshness of a documentary. But it is not. Mr. Yee never knew either man and made up the whole thing.

I can say he hit the nail on the head with some confidence because I did know the real Purdy and the real Acorn and find Mr. Yee's recreation of their carryings-on uncannily true to life. I can picture them and hear them through his lines. It is a warts-and-all portrait to be sure, but it is also an empathetic and heartfelt one. I can imagine Purdy being quite impressed were he somehow able to experience it. He would be especially moved to receive such an insightful tribute from a writer of Asian Canadian ancestry. Acorn would probably find some reason to be outraged. Outrage was his default position.

A play like this has a dual role. One is to bring historic figures and past eras back to life. But another is to create a meaningful story that may or may not have much to do with the real models, and the story Mr. Yee tells here is very much his own creation. He seizes on clues left behind, like the famous Purdy poem "House Guest," to place male friendship under the microscope and explore its rich potential for camaraderie as well as its awkward dead ends. Not incidentally, *among men* also investigates the insecurity and anxiety even major artists struggle with on their road to success.

among men is a thoroughly satisfying work by an impressive voice in Canadian theatre.

As president of Harbour Publishing and Douglas &
McIntyre, Howard White LLD *(Hon.) published over* 1,000
books by Canadian writers, including seven by Al Purdy.
His own books include The Men There Were Then,
Writing in the Rain, Patrick and the Backhoe, The
Sunshine Coast, Airplane Ride, A Mysterious Humming
Noise, *and* Here on the Coast. *He has been awarded the*
Order of British Columbia, the Stephen Leacock Medal
for Humour, and the Order of Canada.

preface

I've always had trouble with men.

By this I mean I have difficulty making friends who are men.
I attribute most of this to being raised by my mother, and to
being a sensitive child. When I was in school, the football guys
totally baffled me. Maybe even scared me a little.[*] I just didn't
understand, what appeared to me, to be the secret language of
maleness. I comprehended even less their fluency in it without
the aid of some Rosetta Stone. Where did this semantic and semi-
otic knowledge stem from? And why was I missing it?

In my junior year, a mutual friend to both me and the team
quarterback unexpectedly died. We happened to pass each other
in the hall just after he'd heard the news. It was during class, so
the halls were empty. I think I had a spare that period. He was
coming down the hall toward me, when suddenly he stopped at
a stairwell door and punched through the door's windowpane. I
called out his name reflexively and he stormed over to me like
I was about to be next. I still didn't know what had happened;
I'd missed the announcement. I was confused and frightened. I
was tall but slight, and here was the star quarterback rushing me
in the hall. I braced myself for violence. Instead, he drew me
into the tightest, most desperate embrace and whispered to me
that our friend was gone. This is the first time I remember being

---

[*] I wasn't bullied or anything. I was on good terms with everyone on account of
being objectively harmless.

physically touched in a platonic* way by another man. I was sixteen years old.

Western culture has been raising touch- and intimacy-averse men since before John Wayne and epitomized by the same. The cultural imagining of "male bonding" brings to mind images of infantile barbarism, and the prospect of men discussing their needs in public has been co-opted by the damaging narratives set forth by assholes like Jordan Peterson.† This culture perpetuates generations of men to accommodate their most difficult emotions with stoicism, emotional withdrawal, and degrees of isolation. In a 2017 *New York Times* article entitled "The Power of Touch, Especially for Men," Andrew Reiner‡ asserts that "the weight of having to suppress stress and the resulting emotions that are perceived as unmanly [. . .] doesn't make men more resilient. It makes them more vulnerable, triggering anxiety and depression."§ Western culture's concept of masculinity has bred a toxicity that has poisoned men's relationship to society and to each other. The "affection deprivation" Kory Floyd describes is "significantly associated with a host of deficits related to general well-being, social well-being, mental health, and physical health" as well as "insecure patterns of interpersonal attachment."¶

As we round out this first quarter of our new century, we find ourselves availed of new language, tools, and resources to

---

* Which is to say this was a touch that was neither violent nor sexual, which are the only two modes of touch men are raised to believe exist.

† Never trust a "Jordan" as they are, categorically, all terrible people.

‡ Referring to the work of psychologist Ofer Zur.

§ Andrew Reiner, "The Power of Touch, Especially for Men," *New York Times*, 12 December 2017, https://www.nytimes.com/2017/12/05/well/family/gender-men-touch.html#:~:text=Touch%20has%20been%20found%2C%20among,critically%2C%20the%20immune%20system's%20resiliency.

¶ Kory Floyd, "Relational and Health Correlates of Affection Deprivation," *Western Journal of Communication*, 78, no. 4 (2014): 383–403.

deconstruct and dismantle old-guard cowboy masculinity. Its toxic effects are being unmasked and confronted, and its prevalence feels in decline. All that being said, while much has been made of calling out and decrying those who enable toxic masculinity, there seems to be little done about actively addressing the narrative among men. While certain behaviour is clearly unacceptable in mixed company, our culture seems satisfied with fear of reprisal as a policing mechanism. The problem with that is that fear has *always* been the primary motivator for men's problematic behaviour: fear of being seen as weak, or the implications that come with emotional vulnerability and sensitivity. Fear is not new. Worse, it's not useful. We need to find ways to normalize affection and intimacy between men in the West. Not in a Seth Rogen/Paul Rudd way, not a "bromance," but an earnest and vital investment in breaking the cycle of affection deprivation.

★ ★ ★

Al Purdy and Milton Acorn were men of a certain era. In their lifetime, they would not see the reckoning coming for the culturally dominant definition of masculinity. Rather, everything in their world was built to enforce and enable it. While neither were saints, nor made claims of being so, their performance of masculinity was tempered by a singular and extraordinary detail: they were poets. They were *sensitive men.** Each embodied the gamut of classical masculine tropes yet were undercut and complicated by their nature as artists, and the most sensitive breed of artist at that. Yes, they were men of a certain time, but they were also men who stood out of time, asynchronous with the world and its populist endeavours.

---

* To use a Purdy-ism from his bar-brawl poem "At the Quinte Hotel."

among men finds Al and Milt at the precipice of success, but still mired in insecurity and poverty. The themes the two poets wrestle with, of success and worth and meaning, are preoccupations of a classical masculine ideal. They are also, intrinsically, preoccupations of an artist's life. The play investigates the process of *building*, of creating something greater than the sum of its parts: a cabin, a poem . . . but, also, a friendship. For me, the question at the heart of this play is *how do we love one another, as men?* How do we express it and what do we need to receive in return, and in what ways?

A Harvard study on happiness has been tracking the lives of nearly eight hundred men[*] over the course of the last eighty-five years. In 2017 they released a report concluding that "close relationships, more than money or fame, are what keep people happy throughout their lives . . . "[†] It's a fun quote to pull out at parties, but it has the added benefit of being true. In which case, the question remains: How? How do men foster these relationships among themselves? How do they decipher the semiotics of masculinity and make substantial, emotional connections? Even if they can manage to get that far, how on earth do they *maintain* those relationships when the dominant constructs of masculinity preclude any innate nurturing instincts? These are the questions I was wrestling with while writing the play. I didn't come up with any answers, but I think it's important to keep asking the questions.

***

---

[*] The study only included men by virtue of it starting in 1938 before women were accepted into the college.

[†] Liz Mineo, "Good Genes are Nice, But Joy is Better," *The Harvard Gazette*, 11 April 2017, https://news.harvard.edu/gazette/story/2017/04/over-nearly-80-years-harvard-study-has-been-showing-how-to-live-a-healthy-and-happy-life/.

Purdy was the first Canadian poet I really took the time to read,[*]
a decision based almost entirely off his epistolary correspondence
with Charles Bukowski, collected in the latter's *Selected Letters*.
Purdy's work, of course, led me to Milton Acorn almost immedi-
ately.[†] Then Birney, Layton, MacEwen, and many of the other
poets mentioned in this play. I burned through Canadian poets,
but always came back to Al and Milt as the ones who spoke to
me the most, in a language I understood. In particular I often
returned to Purdy's poem "House Guest," which is, ostensibly,
a poetic recollection of the period of time Al and Milt were
together in Ameliasburgh building the A-frame cabin that has
since become its own iconic figure. It's the poem that inspired
me to write this play.

What I find striking about "House Guest" is that it doesn't just
capture Al's voice but creates a rather stunning portrait of Milt.
While one can perfectly imagine Al's impish grin while goading
Milt, one conjures with equal clarity Milt's abominable frustra-
tion at being toyed with. While the subjects of their conversations
run pretty fast and loose, the *quality* of their relationship casts a
steady glow over all of it. I felt the entire breadth of their friendship in that one poem.

Al and Milt's poetry resists easy categorization. They were poets
of the people, everymen who embodied a Canadian working class.
They weren't scholars but were exceptionally well versed on a
variety of subjects, especially—in Milt's case—Marxism. In their

---

[*] The first collection of Al's I read was *Rooms for Rent in the Outer Planets*. To
this day, I have two copies of this book. I have no idea why. I can only surmise that
I bought it, never read it, forgot I had it, saw it again at the same bookstore, became
curious all over again, and bought it for—what I thought was—the first time. For
anyone who knows me well, this is fairly classic behaviour. I did the same thing with
Leonard Cohen's *Book of Longing*.

[†] The first collection of Milt's I read was, I believe, *In a Springtime Instant* . . . but it
also might have been *I Shout Love and Other Poems*.

collected works you will find poems about barroom brawls and destitute streets of major cities, alongside heart-wrenching poems of unrequited love, fully realized love turned sour, issues of social justice, and poetic sketches of natural wonder and Canadian wilderness. None of this was accomplished in a vacuum. They travelled the country, lived multihyphenate lives, tried and failed at many things—including poetry—before they came to be the literary lions they are remembered as. Maybe most notably there is a current under all their work, a steady hum of disquiet and longing, of loneliness and of love. Much like their poetry, their character defies easy categorization. They were complicated men. To borrow from Whitman, they contained multitudes.*

We often talk about the absence of a definitive Canadian identity, or a national *voice*, as if it was the thing that holds us back from having a more significant artistic impact on the world. I'm not sure I agree with the assertion that we don't have that. Or, rather, I would offer that our national voice isn't (and shouldn't be) singular, but a chorus. Al and Milt's voices, within that chorus, are emboldened by their predecessors, peers, and proteges. They rise alongside Layton and MacEwen, but also Bliss Carman and (begrudgingly) Robert Service. They rise alongside Ondaatje, Atwood, Carson, Clarke, Brand. Alongside Sze, Thien, and Lau. We are best served by our diversity of voice.

As a country, we also contain multitudes.

***

---

* Walt Whitman, "Song of Myself," in *Leaves of Grass*.

At the risk of this preface being longer than the play it precedes, I've got one last thing, and then I'll go.

As much as this play is an investigation into platonic relationships among men, it is also simply a celebration and an elegy to these extraordinary poets who deserve one more day in the sun. I maintain the importance of keeping these voices and stories alive through our contemporary work, and to include them in our perpetual revisioning of our cultural identity. More broadly, we must also try with all our might to keep *poetry* alive in our minds and our hearts, and to share it across generations.

I started reading poetry in earnest around 2002. I started with Auden, then Eliot and Yeats, then Dickenson, then Spender . . . that was enough to keep me busy for a few years. In 2004 I saw a play by Praxis Theatre at the Toronto Fringe called *Blood of a Coward*, about the life and poetry of Charles Bukowski. That play put me on to Buk, who had endless material to devour, including his *Selected Letters*, which led me to Purdy and, nearly twenty years down the road, to me writing this now. It's not that I was somehow unaware of a culturally ubiquitous poet like Bukowski, but the play made me see his work in a new light. It positioned him in a way I found more accessible at the time.

I think we reject poetry for the same reason we reject religion; we're taught it too early, before we're ready to make meaning of it for ourselves. We learn it by rote or are indoctrinated into it by our parents or education system, which is the best way to ruin anything. Both poetry and religion are at their most potent when we come to them in our own time, our own way. More similarly, each are vital in that they are the last vestiges of the essential questions our culture has gradually, numbly stopped asking: Why are we here? What is the point of us, anyway? What is a life?

I think people quote scripture to bring themselves closer to God. We should quote poetry in service of the same.

∗ ∗ ∗

My wish for this play is that it keeps on living, carrying the voices of Al, Milt, and the rest of the here-contained oft-quoted poets with it. If you see it languishing on a bookshelf or a sale bin at some second-hand store, do me a favour and pick it up. Gift it to a friend or a neighbour. Keep the word moving, changing hands, offering what Auden called those *ironic points of light*[*] flashing out in the darkness of the world.

Thank you for being a part of that process by reading this. Thank you for helping me build something greater than the sum of its parts.

See you in the funny papers.

David Yee
Amalfi Coast, 2023

---

[*] W.H. Auden, "September 1, 1939," in *Another Time*.

among men was first produced by Factory Theatre, Toronto, from April 23 to May 15, 2022, with the following cast and creative team:

Al Purdy: Ryan Hollyman
Milton Acorn: Carlos Gonzalez-Vio

Director: Nina Lee Aquino
Dramaturgy: Matt McGeachy
Set and Costume Design: Joanna Yu
Lighting Design: Michelle Ramsay
Sound Design and Composition: Christopher Stanton
Assistant Director: Cameron Grant
Stage Manager: Tamara Protic
Apprentice Stage Manager: Kayla Ado

characters

Milt
Al

notes

Al Purdy and Milton Acorn were both white men. There's no
getting around it. But that doesn't mean they need to be cast that
way. There was never even a workshop where they were both
played by white actors. While I understand that everyone has
their own casting priorities, I would strongly encourage anyone
thinking of producing this work to not feel burdened by verisimilitude in terms of casting. Nothing would make me happier than
to see this show continue to be cast diversely. And while your job
isn't necessarily to make me happy . . . it also can't hurt.

scene one: Milt's dream

Winter, late evening. 1959. The A-frame at Roblin Lake in Ameliasburgh, Ontario. It is a half-built wooden cabin with a wood-fire stove at its centre, which must be tended so as not to freeze. There is a small kitchen-ette area to one side and a tiny room or two just out of sight. It smells of cedar and cigars, sweat, poverty, and poems. AL Purdy and MILT Acorn, two broke-ass poets who are—in the next ten years—going to be considered the country's greatest poetic forces but are currently just broke-ass men, are drunk and mid-conversation.

MILT: . . . it's unbelievable, this girl, this . . . muse . . . she's kissing me and . . . and touching me.

AL: At the reading?

MILT: *During* the reading! Ondaatje is up there—you know him? young guy, he's okay—reading . . . I don't know, something . . . a bit *flowery*—he's warming up the room, anyway.

AL: And the girl—

MILT: —is rubbing me and kissing my ear, real sexy-like. I'm reading last—they put me last—

AL: *They always put us last . . .*

MILT: —so I know I've got time. There's this Ondaatje kid and Alden is reading from . . . that one about darkness . . . I don't like it, it doesn't *move*, like he's reading a bowl of fruit. The word has got to *move*, Alden, I fucking told the kid—

AL: And the girl—

MILT: —has got her hand on my cock, rubbing me through my pants. I'm in the goddamn front row! I've got this Ondaatje kid going on about . . . mayflies? Dragonflies. I don't—some fucking thing, anyway, and I'm at full mast in the front row thinking, "I'm going to cum in my pants listening to a fucking poem about dragonflies." Or mayflies. Some fucking thing. My worst nightmare.

> *Beat.*

The prosody of the poem is totally off—

AL: And the girl—

MILT: —unzips my fly and I'm powerless. I'm fucking powerless to stop her. My cock's out in front of the literary—the Toronto *poshocracy*—

AL: Who said that?

MILT: "Who said that"—*I* said that.

AL: Whose *word* is that, I mean.

4

MILT: Isherwood.

AL: *(a bit reverently)* Isherwood.

MILT: By way of Auden.

AL: *(more reverently)* Auden . . .

MILT: What was I . . . ?

AL: Your cock was out—

MILT: —and in her mouth! Her head's bobbing up and down like a lake buoy and it was—I don't wanna be uncouth—

    AL *laughs louder.*

—but it was fucking glorious, Al. This was the best— y'know what it felt like?

AL: I imagine it felt like a blow job.

MILT: It felt like I was fucking a honeycomb.

    Beat.

AL: You're going to need to unpack that for me.

MILT: Warm and smooth, waxy almost, but soft . . . this softness that flowed around my cock.

AL: Hexagonal?

MILT: Don't be an asshole.

AL: You sound like Robert Frost doing a bad impression of Dylan Thomas.

MILT: Imposters, both.

AL: *Robert Frost?*

MILT: "The Road Not Taken"? Go fuck yourself.

What was I . . . ?

AL: Honeycomb.

MILT: It was the single most blissful sensation I, or my cock, had ever experienced. Effortless, guiltless pleasure.

AL: *(making a show of his musing)* Is pleasure ever guiltless?

MILT: *(overly disdainful)* Spare me.

> AL *puts up his hands in surrender.*

I'm on the precipice of glory. I don't care that we're at a reading—*my* reading—I don't care that it's the front row or that I can see that arts writer from the *Star* halfway into a paragraph about Milton Acorn getting blown at— I don't care. I drop my head back, I light up a cigar, and blow rings at the ceiling . . . and then I notice something. A shift.

I look down . . . and the girl isn't there. In her place is that *Ondaatje* kid, my cock halfway down *his* throat. The *girl* is now on stage reading his poem about butterflies—

AL: Mayflies.

MILT: Whatever the fuck. But here's the thing: it still *feels amazing*. And *he* doesn't seem to mind, and his poem actually sounds better when *she* reads it. Now—

AL: Hold on. You're saying the Ondaatje kid is blowing you?

MILT: Yah.

AL: Christ, Milt, he's a teenager!

MILT: No! What? No, I forgot to—he's old now. He got old. All of a sudden.

AL: Whatever you say, Nabokov.

MILT: It's a dream, Al. Things like that happen. He's ancient now. He's got a beard, and he's wearing some kind of animal pelt.

AL: Sure.

MILT: *(frustrated)* Can I finish, please?

AL: Is that what you said to him?

MILT: The story, Al. Can I finish the story?

AL waves his hands, gesturing to proceed.

Just as I'm about to release, on death's doorstep, suddenly it's my turn to read. Everyone else has—we've reached the end of the evening and it's my turn to read.

I withdraw myself from the elder Ondaatje's mouth, zip up, and step on stage. I'm still visibly aroused, and my cock gets to the lectern before I do. I knock the goddamn thing over with my giant erection and all the poems flutter and glide to the floor around me. I can't bend over to pick them up for some reason, it made sense at the time.

I'm left standing in front of a room full of people with this massive stiffy and a lit cigar when suddenly it dawns on me that these people all think I'm ugly.

AL: *(with a wink)* You *are* ugly.

MILT: But it's different. They aren't repulsed aesthetically—not *only*, anyway. They revile at what they see *inside* me. Which is, generally speaking, something only *I* do. It's overwhelming, their disgust, it's palpable, and I start to sweat—well, sweat *more*—I can't breathe. It hurts. It physically *hurts*.

My body is urging me to do something, to open my mouth and *speak*. I'd been working on a new poem. I think I can recite it from heart. I just need to open my mouth. So I do.

> *He takes a breath. Maybe a drink. Maybe he lights a cigar.*

I don't know how to describe this next part.

AL: When you recite the poem?

MILT: I don't . . . it's not a poem. What comes out of my mouth . . . it isn't poetry. It's . . . flowers.

A short beat for this to land on AL.

Peonies. Lilacs. Lily of the valley. Orchids. Hydrangeas. Tulips. Geraniums. Thorns scrape my esophagus as an ocean of roses blossoms out of me. Ivy snakes around my face, down my body, and toward the door. "Acorn Blooms at *Moment* Magazine Launch" I somehow know the arts reporter for the *Star* is writing in their little notebook.

I see the girl, from before, the muse of fellatio, standing at the back of the room. She's turned into a giant Venus flytrap, but I know it's her. She's swallowing the young Ondaatje boy (he's young again now), his legs dangle from her mouth for a moment before he's fully masticated.

AL: How curious.

MILT: The next thing I know, the whole room is being stormed by Roman soldiers in full battle armour: the helmets with the broom heads on them. And they're chanting, "Bring us the head of Milton Acorn. Long live Al Purdy."

And then I wake up.

Beat. AL *considers this.* MILT *drinks and smokes. They sit in quiet contemplation for a moment.*

So?

AL: Hm?

MILT: What do you think it means?

Beat. AL *gets up.*

AL: Good night, Milt.

AL *starts heading off to bed.*

MILT: What do you think it means?!

AL: Stoke the fire before you go to sleep and don't drink all the whisky or we'll have to go into town again.

MILT: Al—

AL: Bundle up tonight, there's a cold snap coming in early. And, Milt . . . there's a pot of honey in the kitchen. If you can control yourself, please *try* not to have intercourse with it. Eurithe likes it in her tea.

MILT: C'mon, I told you all of that stuff—that was personal stuff I told you. You can't just go to bed.

AL *stops.*

What do you think it means?

    Beat.

AL: It means . . . *(a mischievous smile)* It means, "Hail Caesar."
Good night.

    AL *disappears into his room and closes the door.* MILT
    is pissed.

MILT: Caesar was assassinated, you know!

    No answer.

They wrote a play about it!

    The light in AL's *room turns off.*

Asshole.

    MILT *puffs on his cigar, pours himself another whisky,*
    leans back in his chair, and closes his eyes. The fire
    burns in the hearth. The fire burns in his heart.

scene two: Prufrock

The next morning. MILT *is up, smoking a cigar, stoking the fire. He recites loudly.*

MILT: "Let us go then, you and I,
When the evening is spread out against the sky
Like a patient etherized upon a table;
Let us go, through certain half-deserted streets,
The muttering retreats
Of restless nights in one-night cheap hotels
And sawdust restaurants with oyster-shells:
Streets that follow like a tedious argument
Of insidious intent
To lead you to an overwhelming question . . .
Oh, do not ask, 'What is it?'
Let us go and make our visit.""

AL comes out of his room, tired and annoyed.

AL: For Christ's sake . . .

MILT: "In the room the women come and go
Talking of Michelangelo."

---

* T.S. Eliot, "The Love Song of J. Alfred Prufrock," *Poetry: A Magazine of Verse* 6, no. 3 (June 1915), 130–35.

AL: It's seven in the goddamn morning.

MILT: "And indeed there will be time
For the yellow smoke—"

AL: No.

MILT: What?

AL: Wrong line.

MILT: "And indeed there will be—"

AL: It's "The yellow fog" yadda yadda . . .

MILT: Is it?

AL: You want coffee?

MILT: Fuck, you're right.

AL: Coffee?

MILT: Yellow fog / yellow smoke . . . fucking hack.

AL: I'll put some on.

> AL *scoops some water out of a pail in the kitchen area
> and starts it boiling.*

"The yellow fog that rubs its back upon the window-panes,
The yellow smoke that rubs its muzzle on the window-panes . . ."

MILT: More words rhyme with "window-panes."

AL: He's doing a thing.

> AL *taps out the meter.*

MILT: Window *frames*, then.

AL: Eh.

MILT: Nursing chains. Velvet cranes. Lions tame.

AL: It's seven in the goddamn morning.

MILT: You make coffee?

AL: Water's on. Would her highness like anything else?

MILT: Christ, Al, it's coffee. I'm not asking for the moon.

> *Beat.*

But if you're offering, I'll take some eggs.

AL: Eggs à la Purdy, coming up.

> AL *goes to the icebox to fetch some eggs.*

MILT: We need a table saw.

AL: *(holding up an egg)* I usually just crack them with a fork.

MILT: For the rafters, ignoramus.

AL: Chuckie at the general store said we could use his saw, but we have to take the beams to him.

MILT: Why can't he bring the saw to us?

AL: I imagine because we're the ones in need of a favour.

MILT: Chuckie's an asshole.

AL: An asshole with a table saw.

MILT: I'll saw them myself.

AL: No you won't.

MILT: You saying I can't do it? I was a carpenter before I met the likes of you.

AL: So you keep saying.

MILT: I'll saw them myself.

AL: Don't be proud.

MILT: It used to be if a man needed a saw, someone in the community would bring that saw to him.

AL: *(in a mocking Russian accent)* Da, comrade Acorn. Let us attack capitalist pig.

MILT: Smart aleck.

AL: Chuckie's a handy type. He needs the saw around. And it's *his*.

MILT: I'll saw them myself, I said.

> AL *serves up the coffee and puts the pot on again for the eggs.*

AL: Coffee.

MILT: Sure.

AL: Make it Irish?

MILT: Wouldn't complain.

> AL *pours a bit of whisky in the mug.*

S'about the only thing that makes your coffee tolerable.

AL: Now you're being unkind.

MILT: Honesty's all we've got, us men.

AL: "Us men"?

MILT: What about it?

AL: You and me?

MILT: Sure.

AL: Apples and oranges.

MILT: Ha!

AL: "Ha"?

MILT: Quit doin' that. Aping me like that. I don't like it.

AL: We're different sorts, is all.

MILT: Still men. Poets. Poor. Salt of the earth, the two of us.

AL: I suppose.

MILT: We're both military men. That's something.

AL: "Military men"?

MILT: Come off it. We served in the war.

AL: You got blown up in the middle of the ocean *on your way* to war. You got deaf because you're too stupid to cover your ears around bombs, so they sent you home. And by the time *I* was done *not* flying in the Air Force, they'd stripped my rank lower than a civilian.

    Beat. MILT *raises his glass.*

MILT: To peace.

AL: To peace.

> *They drink.*

MILT: Eurithe drink your coffee?

AL: She does.

MILT: No complaints?

AL: None that I hear.

MILT: Either that woman's a saint, or you and me have a deafness in common.

AL: Could be both.

MILT: It's wretched coffee, Al.

AL: Good morning to you, too.

> *Beat.* MILT *remembers something and fishes out an envelope to hand to* AL.

MILT: You got a letter.

AL: You've been to town? How early do you wake up?

MILT: *(coughs guilty)* Couple days ago.

AL: Couple days?

MILT: Five, maybe.

AL: Waiting for a special occasion, were you?

MILT: It got a little misplaced. I put it in my pocket, and then I put my pocket somewhere. Or, the pants. You know what I mean.

AL: *(looks at the letter)* This is . . . I've been waiting for this letter! This is the CBC letter I've been waiting on.

MILT: Well, then, you're welcome.

AL: You *lost* it.

MILT: Well I *found* it again, didn't I?

AL: Unbelievable.

MILT: And don't yell so early. You're ruining a perfectly bucolic morning! Scared all the damn birds away. You had a goldfinch there and now he's flown off to Belleville where people are fucking civilized.

> AL *has stopped listening and opens the letter.*

Well? Are you rich and famous? You gonna write for *Cannonball*?

> *Beat.* AL *crumples up the letter. His heart breaks a little and his shoulders slump. He turns his attention back to the eggs.* MILT *softens a bit.*

19

Just as well. Fame would go to your head anyway.

Beat.

The show is pretty socialist, when you think about it, *Cannonball*. Coupl'a truckers, working-class guys, having adventures. Heroes of the proletariat. The bad guys are always the establishment, the suits. But they get redeemed, too, because . . . y'know . . .

He gestures something with his hands.

Canada.

Beat.

I like the young guy. William Campbell? I saw him in a play a year or two ago. He's pretty good. But the older guy, the guy who plays Cannonball, what's his name?

Nothing.

He seems like he might murder someone with little to no provocation.

I bet he has. I bet he's murdered someone. A neighbour, maybe. Someone ethnic. A Polish neighbour! I can see it in his eyes. He thinks about it while he's acting those scenes, driving that truck. The memory of the time he had a dead Polish neighbour in his trunk and he buried him in a ravine. The stench of death and cabbage rolls fresh in his memory. I can see it all. He's a menace. A goddamn menace.

Beat. An idea.

We should solve mysteries!

AL cracks a smile despite himself.

We'll travel from town to town across the Pacific Northwest and solve mysteries while living off the land. Writing poems and pinning them to the criminals we catch, leaving them hog-tied in front of rural police stations. Folk singers will write ballads about us. Children will play-act our adventures in front yards with sticks for guns, reciting our poems.

Our most famous case will, of course, be nabbing the lead actor of CBC television's hit show *Cannonball*: Johnnie Murder-Eyes. We'll get him right before he stabs his new neighbour: a Tunisian insurance salesman.

Beat. Still nothing.

This, naturally, leads to us being crowned Tunisian princes and marrying—

AL: *(cracking, finally and good-naturedly)* Okay! Enough!

MILT laughs, victorious. Short beat.

MILT: Public broadcasters should stick to educational programming. Leave artistic merit to the poets.

AL waves his hand in the air.

AL: It's fine.

MILT: *Bureaucracy* is what it is! No place in *art* for bureaucracy!

AL: Okay, okay.

MILT: Who are they to say what's art and what isn't?

AL: Who are we to say the same?

MILT: We're artists!

AL: That doesn't mean a goddamn thing and you know it. If we start drawing lines that way, then we make art . . . drama . . . poetry an esoteric thing. If we are the great deciders, then we're nothing more than the elite. We're no better than the TISH boys in godforsaken Vancouver.

MILT: I'm not saying the *elite* . . .

AL: Lord knows that would upset the tiny Soviet who lives inside you and pulls the strings to make you move around.

MILT: What are you saying now?

AL: *(yells into MILT's mouth)* Make him dance, Vladimir!

MILT: You're a crackpot.

AL: It's *fine*, Milt. They didn't like the play. That's *fine*. It's a shit bit of luck, but I can't say they're wrong about it because they were *right* about it when they accepted the last one. And I can't

. . . I can't go around saying that I'm *better* than they are, because what's wrong with the world is that every asshole thinks he's better than every other asshole.

They didn't like it. Fine. But we are not counterweights on the scale of lesser art.

    Beat.

MILT: When you're done moralizing, can I say one thing?

AL: I'm in no mood for this, Milt.

MILT: Just one thing.

AL: Sure. Fine. What?

MILT: You *do* think you're better than everyone! You say it all the goddamn time how much better you are than everyone! You walk around here like you're Arturo fucking Bandini: you wrote "The Little Dog Laughed"! But the minute someone knocks you down a peg, you turn into Saint fucking Purdy. "It's not for us to say" is a bullshit excuse to feel sorry for yourself.

I'm not saying we're the goddamn elite. I'm saying that a car collector is not the same as a mechanic. If you're going to appraise something, you need to know the guts of it.

    Beat.

AL: What did *you* think of it?

Short pause.

You read it, the night you came up here. I saw you sitting with the carbon, right there. So what did *you* think of it?

Beat. MILT *is caught. He tries to brush it off.*

MILT: Ah, what do I know?

AL's had it. He grabs his jacket and shoes, hastily pulling on a hat.

AL: I'm going to town.

MILT: Don't be like that.

AL: Saw the goddamn rafters if you're doing it.

MILT: Al . . .

AL: I'll be back later.

AL storms out, slamming the door behind him. Beat. MILT *looks toward the kitchen.*

MILT: I'll just make my own eggs, then. Fucking baby.

He just stares at the eggs, not really keen to do it. Not really keen to do much but smoke his cigar. He picks up a book and starts reading.

scene three: stoking the fire

Later that evening. From off, the voices of MILT *and* AL
are heard as they try to place the newly sawed rafters.
They are drunk and on ladders.

AL: You measure this right?

MILT: Don't start with me, Al.

AL: It doesn't fit!

MILT: It fits. You just gotta put your back into it.

AL: We should rotate it.

MILT: It's a goddamn *square*—it won't matter if you rotate it.

AL: How do you know this is the top?

MILT: It's a rafter. There's no top or bottom, it's the same on all
sides.

AL: There's always a top and a bottom.

MILT: Says who?

AL: Chuckie said.

MILT: Chuckie the saw-hoarding asshole?

AL: One and the same.

MILT: That guy doesn't know what he's talking about.

AL: We should rotate it.

MILT: Stop that!

AL: I think this is the bottom.

MILT: Quit turning it!

AL: Don't yank it like that!

MILT: *You* don't yank it like—

> *The sound of a large piece of lumber hitting the floor.*

God*DAMMIT.*

> AL *is laughing hysterically.* MILT *comes into the main room. He's dusty and his hand is cut. He's mad as hell. After a moment,* AL *follows, still laughing.*

Oh shut up, will ya?

AL: I told you not to yank the damn thing!

MILT: I got a fucking splinter 'cause of you.

> AL *holds up his hand—he's also bleeding. He can barely breathe he's laughing so hard.*

AL: Me too.

> MILT *scowls, looks at* AL's *hand. Then he starts laughing too. They're both howling, rolling on the floor.* MILT *takes* AL's *hand, grabs the splinter between his fingers, and pulls it out.* AL *yelps in pain, then collapses laughing again.* MILT *holds out his hand to* AL.

MILT: Do mine! Do mine!

> *With the grace of an elephant,* AL *rips the splinter out of* MILT's *hand.* MILT *howls in pain.* MILT *grabs the whisky and takes a shot, then pours some on his hand.* AL *does the same. They're screaming in pain, then laughter, then pain again. Finally they collapse on the floor next to each other, staring up at the A-frame roof. They breathe. The ice on the lake cracks.* MILT *lights a cigar. He blows rings at the ceiling and conjures a poem.*

It's the last stormtime of winter. As if the ghosts of ancestors
Forgetting even they are ancestors
Were wandering. They cannot groan so the trees groan for them;
The hiss of the snows is their wordless breath.[*]

---

[*]   Milton Acorn, "It's the Last Stormtime," in *More Poems for People* (Toronto: NC Press, 1972), 26.

Beat.

AL: You always gotta ruin a goddamn moment, don't you?

MILT laughs.

I like it. You should write it down.

MILT: I'll remember it. I remember the good ones.

AL: Well, that should be easy. There being so few of them.

MILT reaches over and punches AL *in the balls.* AL *groans. Beat.*

"Over the rim of a lacquered bowl,
Where a cold blue water-color stands
I see the wintry breakers roll
And heave their froth up the freezing sands.

Here in immunity safe and dull,
Soul treads her circuit of trivial things.
There soul's brother, a shining gull,
Dares the rough weather on dauntless wings."[*]

MILT inhales thoughtfully.

MILT: Is that . . . Bliss Carman?

AL: It most definitely *is*.

---

[*]   Bliss Carman, "A Winter Piece," in *Later Poems* (Toronto: McClelland & Stewart, 1921), 166.

MILT *laughs uproariously.*

MILT: What the hell are you doing with *Bliss Carman* in your head?

AL: Oh, you never know who's running around in there.

MILT: He was a Maritimer, y'know?

AL: I'm well aware.

MILT: A herring choker.

AL: You got a quaint old nickname for everything out there, don't you?

MILT: What of it?

AL: Buncha Dr. Seuss–loving drunks, you islanders.

MILT: Yer make me right owly if y'keep on like that.

AL *laughs.*

AL: You hear the one about the woman who moved to PEI when she was one year old? Never left, lived her entire life there, died in her nineties. Her obituary read: "Woman from *away* dies peacefully at residence."

MILT *laughs. Beat.*

MILT: S'getting cold. We need wine or wood.

AL: Wine's empty.

MILT: Wood, then. Where do you keep it?

>AL *stares at him.*

AL: What do you mean where do I keep it?

MILT: Where do you keep your firewood?

AL: You mean the firewood I asked you to take in from the pile outside and stack by the door because it was going to snow all day? Where do I keep *that* firewood?

>*They look to the door. No wood. Outside, an icy, frozen winterscape.*

MILT: Hm.

AL: Oh Christ. You left it outside.

MILT: It wasn't snowing *all* day. It warmed up.

AL: And then it *rained*. After which the wind picked up and it all froze.

MILT: *Force majeure.* We're helpless to the elements.

AL: Which is why you bring it *inside*!

MILT: Okay, already. I said "sorry," didn't I?

Beat.

AL: No. *You didn't.*

MILT: I'm sure I meant to.

AL: Milton Acorn, as a poet you are—undoubtedly—one of the finest. But as a *person*, you are an abject fucking failure.

Beat.

MILT: You really think I'm one of the finest?

AL rolls over and punches MILT in the balls. MILT howls.

AL: We're going to freeze to death.

MILT: You Ontario boys always think you're going to freeze to death.

AL: There is one very large block of wood that's still dry.

MILT: Oh yah?

It dawns on him.

Oh no. No. *No.* I just sawed that rafter—we're not chopping it into kindling.

AL: Maybe it'll fit, then.

MILT: You go near that beam and I'll knock you out, boy.

> AL *looks around. He grabs yesterday's newspaper and starts separating pages out.*

AL: Okay, twist these up nice and tight. The denser they are, the longer they'll burn.

MILT: What section do we start with?

> *Beat.*

BOTH: Arts.

> *They start tearing out pages and twisting them into large matchsticks.*

MILT: Save me that page, will ya? I haven't done the crossword yet.

AL: Yes, by all means, *that* should be your primary concern.

MILT: Comics are on the reverse side.

AL: Okay, we'll save that page.

MILT: Love that *Peanuts* gang, don't you?

AL: We all have our vices.

MILT: Classifieds next.

> MILT *starts pulling them out and twisting them up.*

AL: Look for a job while you're at it.

MILT: *(scanning through)* I shoulda been a die maker.

AL: There's still time.

MILT: I could be a taxi driver.

AL *laughs.*

AL: You don't have the temperament.

MILT: Like you would know.

AL: I'll have you know I *ran* a taxi company, in Belleville.

MILT: *(scoffs)* What were you, head poet?

AL: Eurithe's father and I bought the outfit, together, after the war.

MILT: I knew I smelled establishment on you.

AL *laughs*

AL: I don't know about that. I was in charge, sure, but— it was this small rinky little operation. We ran it out of our apartment, Eurithe and me. I had a half-dozen cars, a dozen or so medallions. Ran the thing for three years.

MILT: G'wan.

AL: This was the precipice of the Bad Times, you understand. The sort of era in a man's life marked entirely by deep significance or profound regret. It all went sideways, everything: the business, the marriage. Eurithe and I split sometime near the end, I don't even recall when or why. But I remember with perfect clarity the look she would give me, night and day, the icicles in her eyes. I loved her so wantonly, and she just . . . despised me. Utter contempt. I must've been awful, but I don't remember it. Sure, I'd bawl her out and she'd do the same to me, but I don't recall *being* monstrous.

MILT: Selective memory. I've got it, too. You worked it out, though.

AL: She's as good of a woman as God ever made. For some unfathomable reason, she chooses to be with me. And one of these days, I'm going to stop holding that against her.

MILT: Yah. Me too.

AL *grins, drunkenly.*

AL: Here's how bad it got. Around '48, she's been gone a year. I'm at a fever pitch. Like there's a fault line that runs through my life and it's forever vibrating, shaking everything loose, sending it down into some dark chasm. The taxi — Diamond Taxi, that was the name — we're in debt to the tits. We're writing IOUs for gasoline, delaying paycheques, creditors on the phone, creditors in the mail, creditors at the door. Life is costing more than it's paying.

It all comes down to this one night, Highway 62 in red October.* The bank's started seizing it all: the cars, the licences, the

---

* Al Purdy, "My Grandfather's Country," in *Wild Grape Wine* (Toronto: McClelland and Stewart, 1968), 125.

goddamn clocks off the walls. I'm driving the last unseized car, a '46 Dodge in tan. It's nighttime, and I don't have a passenger, you understand. I'm just *driving*. I get convinced, somehow, that the car behind me is one of the bailiffs they send to repossess assets. It looked like one of their cars, I'd seen 'em enough. Thinking about it now, I don't really know if it was them or just some guy who'd forgotten where he lived after a couple of beers at the Quinte. I was trying to outrun him. Trying to outrun . . . all of it. Making wild turns, turning off the lights to evade detection, speeding down straightaways . . . and then I get to this hill.

I drive up, and I'm at a lookout point, some place you might go as teenagers to get lucky. Maybe I'd even been there, back in the RCAF days, I don't know. The important thing is that the hill is maybe fifty feet above a small lake. It's a pretty night with a harvest moon. I got out, found a rock to put on the gas pedal . . . and I just sent that '46 Dodge in tan straight into the lake.

Better she should have it than some fucking creditor.

Took longer to go under than I thought it would. Finished a bottle of Black Label and half a beer before the tail lights disappeared under the water.

Still, nothing felt . . . lighter. Which was maybe what I was expecting, I don't know. I took a long walk back to the 401 and hitched to Toronto. There was nothing left for me in Belleville. No business, no Eurithe. Just angry phone messages and unopened, stern-faced mail.

Beat. MILT *holds up a section of the newspaper.*

MILT: Sports section?

AL: Save the highlights. Burn the rest.

He does.

AL *reaches over to grab a bound stack of carbons from a table.*

Take this, too.

MILT *takes it. Curious, he peeks at it.*

MILT: Come off it, Al.

AL: What?

MILT: I'm not burning your play.

AL: Well *some* good should come of it.

MILT: You're being petty.

AL: I'm not trying to be petty. I'm trying to be *warm*.

MILT: I'll let us both die of exposure before I burn any of your goddamn writing.

AL: I can't say I'll be as magnanimous, so if you've got any copies of *In Love and Anger*, lemme have 'em.

MILT *glares at him.*

36

See, *now* I'm being petty. So you can spot the difference later.

> *Beat.*

MILT: We've all been let down by it, you know. All been in the shit. Tasted our own blood. None of us are special for it.

AL: Spare me the pep talk.

MILT: Spare me the sooking, then.

AL: The word is "sulking."

MILT: The word is "go fuck yourself."

> AL *laughs.*

Look at us. Not a dollar or a diploma between us, drunk off whisky and wild grape wine, freezing slowly to death in the middle of fucking nowhere Prince Edward Cunty, steps from the historic, uh . . .

AL: Roblin Lake Mill.

MILT: The historic Roblin Lake Mill, where nothing of historical value ever fucking happened. In a wasteland devoid of culture, not a library or a good-looking girl in sight. Two men who write poems, sensitive men . . . building a house. A *house*, Al.

Where did you even get the goddamn idea for a *house*?

AL: We saw it in a magazine.

MILT: Dreamers, Al. Coupl'a dreamers. Building a house.

AL's getting sleepy. He yawns a bit.

AL: Eurithe honestly built most of it.

MILT laughs.

She's a handy woman.

MILT: But who'll get all the credit?

AL: Alfred Wellington Purdy. I wrote "The Little Dog Laughed."

MILT laughs.

MILT: We let down and we get let down. No one ever gets their due, that's fantasy. Pixie dust. Meritorious academic bullshit. We let down and we get let down. Tasting our own blood.

AL: "The lyf so short, the craft so long to lerne."*

MILT: *(appreciatively)* Hmmm.

AL: Burn the play, Milt.

MILT: I won't do it.

AL: It's bad.

---

* Geoffrey Chaucer, *Parlement of Foules*, 1.

MILT: It's not bad.

AL: Worse than that. It's ordinary.

MILT: Doesn't mean you have to torch it. .

AL: Maybe if it really *is* good then it won't burn. Like a Salem witch. Give it a shot, then.

MILT: You're drunk.

AL: I'm not drunk. I'm having a momentary lapse of sobriety. I'll feel the same way about it in the morning.

MILT: Then we'll burn it in the morning.

AL: We'll be frozen stiff by then.

MILT: And you, immortalized in your final playscript.

AL: The CBC'll have it, then. They're more interested in you after you're dead. Like worms.

> *MILT blindly grabs a handful of mail and sorts through it.*

MILT: While I refuse to commit your words to the pyre, I've no compunction about the work of lesser authors.

> *Sifting through.*

You and your letters. One from Dudek, unopened. Layton, unopened.

AL: I've been busy. Building a house, if you hadn't noticed.

MILT: Birney, opened. He's sent you some poems. They look particularly flammable.

AL: Don't you dare. Earle Birney walks on water. Give it here.

> *MILT hands the letter over and moves on to another one.*

MILT: Oh, the young and prodigious Mr. Curt Lang has sent you some poems.

AL: Don't be obstinate.

MILT: Did Lowry really call him "the most promising writer since Shakespeare"?

AL: You were *at* that party, Milt.

MILT: I was? I don't recall.

AL: You were drunk. So was Lowry. So was I, come to think of it. In any case, he isn't. Or maybe he is. He's a good kid, anyway.

MILT: He needs about twenty more years on him before he can lay the line down.

AL: Oh yah? How many more years do *we* need?

MILT: 'Bout the same.

They laugh.

He's a gregarious sort, though. Don't trust that about a man. People always flocking to him like he's got the answers to a pop quiz.

AL *shrugs.*

AL: He's tall. Handsome.

MILT: We'll only ever know half of that equation.

AL: Speak for yourself. I'm gorgeous.

MILT laughs.

MILT: Oh yah, the ladies love a forehead that reaches all the way back to your ass.

AL: Says the guy who looks like a wax figure of himself.

MILT growls.

Burn the Lang poems.

MILT: Aha! I knew he wasn't Shakespeare.

AL: He's got a couple good poems. He just hasn't written them yet.

MILT: Hack.

AL: Be generous.

MILT: That *is* generous. What I *really* think is that he's an asshole.

> *MILT crumples up the poems and tosses them in the fire. He sorts through more mail.*

What's this?

> *He hands AL a flyer.*

AL: That's the newsletter from what's-his-name. I don't know how he got my address. Just pitch it.

> *MILT reads it with some interest.*

MILT: Ryerson Press is reissuing his chapbook.

AL: Unbelievable. You want to feed Birney poems to the stove, but the *newsletter* is worth reading.

MILT: *(ignoring him)* There's a poetry conference at Queen's. Next month.

AL: Ugh. Can't stand those things.

MILT: Yah.

AL: Academic troglodytes with their Macallan 12s and PhDs.

MILT: Oughta be some poets there, still.

AL: Critics, mostly.

MILT: Still . . .

AL: *(sensing something)* Go if you like. It's not far.

MILT: Me? *(scoffs)* No.

AL: *(gently encouraging)* They'd be excited to have you. The carpenter poet, Milton Acorn, gracing their lectern. Read them some *real* poetry—poetry of the people.

MILT: They wouldn't know who I was.

AL: Sure they would. You're Arturo fucking Bandini.

MILT: Hah.

> AL *yawns. He gets closer to sleep with every passing moment.*

AL: You're a fine poet, Milt. A fine poet. A disaster of a personality and a monstrosity to look at. You snore like a Gatling gun, and you have the manners of a street urchin. You smoke too much, drink too much, talk too much about bullshit and too little about anything that matters. They'd be happy to see you. Mainly because they've never met you. But also because you are a fine poet. A damn fine one.

If I'm honest . . . and that's a big if, mind you . . . you're a better poet than me.

Beat. He's halfway asleep.

But Christ are you ever ugly.

He starts to snore lightly.

MILT *puts a blanket over* AL. *He folds up the newsletter and puts it in his pocket. He props himself up and lights a cigar. He stares off into the dark, the fading light of the last Douglas fir embers in the stove casting a glow on his face.*

MILT: "When the great wind comes
and the robberies of the rain
you stand on the corner shivering.
The people who go by—
you wonder at their calm.

They miss the whisper that runs
any day in your mind,
'Who are you really, wanderer?'—
and the answer you have to give
no matter how dark and cold
the world around you is:
'Maybe I'm a king.'"*

He falls asleep, cigar snug between his fingers. The fire burns miraculously on.

---

* William Stafford, "A Story that Could be True," in *Stories That Could be True* (New York: Harper & Row, 1977), 4.

scene four: dynamite

*A typewriter clacking away at dawn. A bit more work
has been done on the A-frame, including the addition
of this typer.* MILT *is sitting at it, punching away at
the keys. He grins as he knocks out the last line, then
reads what he's got aloud. As he does,* AL *stumbles in,
tired and grumpy.* MILT *doesn't notice him.*

MILT: "Smoke and in a blue halo let a poem grow
Of winter and sky blue as laughter
Tinting immaculate snow,
The crows fasting on their pine pulpits
And all the other birds gone, except
On a white tablecloth of snow,
The chickadees, happy and fat as a chuckle"*

     Beat.

Hm.

     AL *crosses to make coffee.*

---

*   Milton Acorn, "Winter Boarders," in *I Shout Love and Other Poems* (Toronto: Aya Press, 1987), 54.

AL: Put that in the shitter when you're done, I want to wipe my ass with it.

MILT: *(turning to see him)* C'mon, now!

AL: "White tablecloth of snow"?

MILT: I'm not settled on it.

AL: You're wasting good paper.

MILT: *You're* wasting good *air*.

AL: It doesn't scan.

MILT: It does!

AL: Not well.

MILT: Enter Alfred Purdy, arbiter of prosody.

AL: *(examining the typewriter)* You're killing the ribbon.

MILT: It's *seven* lines!

AL: You're giving the ribbon bad taste. You're training it to write bullshit. Before you know it, it'll type George Bowering poems all by itself.

MILT: You're some kind of misery this morning.

AL: I used to wake up to the birds chirping, Milt. I used to wake up to the gentle scraping of deer rubbing their antlers on the trees. But for the last month I wake up to either your snoring or your goddamn soliloquizing, both of which drag the nails half out the walls in either demonic percussion or masturbatory vociferation. The only reason I get out of bed half the time is the overwhelming urge to *murder you in cold blood where you stand*.

Do you want eggs?

MILT: Yes, please.

    AL goes to the icebox to get eggs.

AL: If you want, you can set places. Just put the "tablecloth of snow" down so we don't sully the wood.

MILT: You're an asshole.

    MILT starts clearing the table to set it for breakfast.

And you're too clever for your own good, you know that? That's what stops you from being a great poet.

AL: And here I thought it was the lack of great poems.

MILT: That, too.

    Beat.

AL: I don't mean it needs to *scan*, iambically or anything—I don't mean *meter*.

MILT: You don't?

AL: The musicality and the syntax are at war with each other. The images are both common and improbable: "blue as laughter," "fat as a chuckle." You use "snow" twice in seven lines.

MILT: But what you said was it didn't *scan*.

AL: The *heart* doesn't scan, Milt. What I mean is the *journey*. I mean . . . I mean where are *you* in this? The "crows fasting on pine pulpits," that's the edge of you, the surface . . . but even that is fleeting. It doesn't scan because it isn't honest.

    Beat. MILT *sets the table.* AL *cooks. All is quiet. Then:*

MILT: Live with me on Earth among red berries and the
    bluebirds
And leafy young twigs whispering
Within such little spaces, between such floors of green,
    such figures in the clouds
That two of us could fill our lives with delicate wanting:

Where stars past the spruce copse mingle with fireflies
Or the dayscape flings a thousand tones of light back at the sun—
Be any one of the colours of an Earth lover;
Walk with me and sometimes cover your shadow with mine.*

---

*   Milton Acorn, "Live With Me on Earth," in *More Poems for People* (Toronto: NC Press, 1973), 10.

Beat. AL *smiles. Inside, he is beaming with pride and jealousy, but he puts a lid on it.*

AL: You should write that one down.

MILT: *(smiling)* I'll remember it. I remember the good ones.

He's happier now, almost dancing as he sets the table.

How are you doing those eggs?

AL: Poached.

MILT: You're a sadist.

AL: What, in the name of all that is holy, is wrong with poached eggs now?

MILT: Hallmark of the upper class.

AL: Eggs are not classist!

MILT: Eggs are *fundamentally* classist. And poached? Poached!

MILT *pulls on his cigar revolutionarily.*

AL: Poached eggs are bourgeois?

MILT: I want a working man's egg. I want an *over easy* egg.

AL: Christ's sake . . .

MILT: It goes:

> *MILT gestures the levels with his hand, going from bottom to top:*

Over easy.
Sunny side up.
Scrambled.

AL: I should never have asked.

MILT: Hard boiled.
Omelette—

AL: What kind of omelette?

MILT: *Every* kind of omelette.

AL: Does that include a frittata?

MILT: That's not a real thing.

AL: What?

MILT: You're making stuff up to get a rise out of me.

AL: A frittata is an open-faced omelette.

MILT: Sounds lazy.

AL: It's Italian.

MILT: Where was I?

AL: Omelette.

MILT: Omelette.
Soft boiled.
Then poached.

AL: You don't think you're attaching too much importance
to eggs?

MILT: You don't think you're attaching too little?

AL: What about a quiche? Or a soufflé?

MILT: Quit making things up, Al.

AL: A quiche is . . . you know what, never mind. It'd be wasted on
you, anyway.

> *Beat.*

Who's that about?

> *MILT shoots him a look.*

"Live with me on Earth."

> *MILT grumbles.*

MILT: Nobody. Doesn't matter.

AL: Sure it matters.

MILT: Does it make it a better poem if you know? If she's real, even? You know better than that. We are neither biographers or verisimilitude artists. We're poets. Is "The Second Coming" a better poem knowing it's about Yeats becoming a father and not the Anglo–Irish war?

AL: What are you on about, now?

MILT: You don't know this?

Good old Billy Butler never wanted kids. His whole life he was dead against it. You can't blame him, looking at the world. But then he marries Georgie. He'd been seduced into this whole mysticism thing, spirits and seances . . . and Georgie, she's a medium. She's got *powers*, right? She knows he doesn't want kids, but thinks to herself, "Fuck it, I can convince him."

AL: Sounds familiar.

MILT: So Georgie starts having these "visions," yah? She tells Bill it's come to her in a dream that they are destined to have a child. The universe, or whatever, has deemed it so. Our boy Yeats balks at this, but Georgie doubles down. She says, "Our child will be the rebirth of the Messiah."

The second coming of Christ.

And because Bill believes her and all that spooky bullshit, he relents. Georgie gets pregnant, and as the child grows inside her, so does fear inside him. What if this child really is the Messiah?

Or what if it's not? What if it's the Devil? Or, worse, what if it isn't either? What if he's been bamboozled? The poem ends with:

" . . . now I know
That twenty centuries of stony sleep
Were vexed to nightmare by a rocking cradle,
And what rough beast, its hour come round at last,
Slouches towards Bethlehem to be born?"*

That's what "The Second Coming" is about.

> *Beat.*

Is it *also* about the Irish War of Independence? Sure, why not.

AL: And you're asking does it make it a better poem, knowing that? Of course it does! Significantly better!

MILT: Ah shit, maybe it does. I don't know, I never liked that poem.

AL: So who's the woman?

MILT: Mind your goddamn business. Where are my eggs?

> AL *serves up the eggs. Coffee, too. They sit at the table and eat, ruminating and drinking coffee in gulps.*

AL: Is it Angie? The . . . what was she, the nurse?

---

* W.B. Yeats, "The Second Coming," in *The Collected Poems of W.B. Yeats* (London: Wordsworth Editions, 2000), 159.

MILT: These are over medium.

AL: Not Rita from the post office.

MILT: I like 'em runnier than this.

AL: You know who fancies you? Gwen MacEwen. She was at that Contact Press reading.

MILT: *(evasive)* There were lots of people there.

AL: Her and Eurithe had a little tête-à-tête about you. She said you two met outside, prior to the reading.

MILT: The trick is you gotta let the whites fully set, and you seal the yolk in but you don't fully cook it.

AL: *(in mock confidence)* Eurithe said . . . that Gwen said . . . that you were very charming.

MILT: *(despite himself)* She did?

> *MILT coughs.*

AL: Oh yes. *Very* charming. So the question is: Who was she talking to? Because that doesn't sound like you.

MILT: Are you yanking my chain?

AL: Remind me where sunny side up falls on Acorn's Hierarchy of Eggs.

MILT: *(dismissively)* Right after over easy.

A *breath*.

Did she really say that?

AL: Why *after* over easy? What makes them more bourgeois than —

MILT: *(getting mad)* Sunny side up has a degree of *fashion* to it, an *aesthetic* versus a utilitarian appeal. Now shut the fuck up and tell me what she said.

AL: *(innocently)* Who?

MILT: I will beat you to death with your own feet, Alfred Purdy.

AL: I just remembered something.

Brief pause.

The hydro is going in tomorrow and I still have to put the pole up.

AL *gets up and throws his boots on.*

MILT: You do this just to make me angry. I know you do.

AL: I got a foot down digging the hole for it and I hit limestone.

He digs something out of a burlap bag by the door.

So I went to Doug's in town and got something to take care of it.

He unravels a stick of dynamite and holds it up so
MILT *can see.*

MILT: What's that?

AL: Dynamite! Catch!

He throws it to MILT, *who dives for cover instead of*
catching it. The stick bounces behind the table.

MILT: What the hell are you doing?!

AL *goes to retrieve the dynamite and waves it at* MILT
jokingly.

AL: Oh it's fine. Doug said it's harmless so long as you don't light
the fuse.

MILT: Stop holding it so close to the stove.

AL *is, in fact, dangerously close to the stove. He waves*
it around the fire like a fool kid with firecrackers.

AL: What, like this? Don't do this? Is this not safe?

AL *laughs.* MILT *steams.*

MILT: You oughta be careful with that stuff.

AL: I suppose I just put it in the hole, light the fuse, and take shelter? Is that how it works?

MILT: How should I know?

AL: Well, you worked around explosives in the war. You've got some limited experience with depth charges. Figured it's a transferable skill.

MILT: The bulk of what I know about explosives is that you have to remember to cover your ears, and I learned that the hard way.

> AL *salutes, heading out the door, throwing the dynamite up in the air and catching it like a baton, over and over.*

AL: Cover your ears. Got it. You wanna come watch?

MILT: No thank you.

> AL *is gone.* MILT *clears the dishes. As he does, he remembers and recites.*

"Live with me on Earth under the invisible daylight moon
Both its face and its shadow gone but it's still there;
Tide-rise and tide-fall, obedience which is not obedience
    but just what it is:
Where thoughts and actions appropriate to a man

Rise amid the welter of winter storms
    —the storms of his words, the grey nul-calm
        of his winter mind—
Where the pages of a book by Irving Layton
Or any other poet who has forgotten
Flutter—unlike a butterfly tethered with a thread."*

---

*   Milton Acorn, "Live With Me on Earth," in *More Poems for People* (Toronto: NC Press, 1973), 10.

AL comes back in. MILT shuts up.

That's the quietest dynamite on the market.

AL: It didn't work.

MILT: Whadd'ya mean it didn't work?

AL: I threw her in, took shelter, plugged my ears . . . no kablam. I thought maybe I just plugged my ears really well and—I don't know—missed it? You didn't hear anything?

MILT: Not a peep.

AL: That's disconcerting.

MILT: Did you look in the hole?

AL: I didn't want to blow my face off. Will you go look?

MILT: So I can blow *my* face off?

AL: It's less of a loss for you.

MILT shoots him a look.

Fine. I'll go look.

AL goes back outside. A moment. Then, from off:

It's just sitting there.

MILT: Did the fuse go out?

AL: The fuse is gone!

Short pause.

Should I grab it? Reach in and grab it?

MILT: I don't know.

AL: I'd rather not.

AL *comes back inside.*

This was a bad idea from the start, if I'm honest.

MILT: The fuse probably just fizzed out before it hit the blasting cap. So there's still a little bit of fuse left . . . just not enough to light it ourselves and get out with all our fingers.

AL: Problematic.

MILT: We could fill the hole with newspaper and light that on fire . . . then that will light the remainder of the fuse and . . .

AL: Kablam.

MILT: Kablam.

They nod and each grab some newspaper, twisting them into sticks as before.

AL: I'm beginning to see why mastery of fire was so important to paleolithic man. It really does come in handy.

They twist newspaper in relative silence. MILT sets one sheet aside. AL raises an eyebrow.

MILT: Crossword.

AL nods. They twist more.

AL: You should ask her out. When you get back to Toronto.

MILT: Who?

AL: "Who." Audrey Hepburn. Who do you think?

MILT: Gwen?

AL nods. MILT wrings his hands, an anxious trait since his youth. That and being punched in the face.

She's half my age.

AL: Doesn't stop the rich guys. Why should it stop you?

MILT: I don't know.

AL: I've known you three years now, Milt. I've never seen you with anyone longer than an evening. You're always lumbering around in that godawful coat—have you ever washed that coat?—with your cigars and your declarations. You write bullshit poetry about nature and, sometimes, exceptional poetry that is so restrained in its pursuit of love. No, restrained is wrong. *Afraid*. Afraid of even speaking the word aloud. Apologizing for loving or needing love. You scream about every other goddamn thing, but you *whisper* about love.

Eurithe thinks you're ashamed. Ashamed of needing . . . thinking it's some sort of weakness. But I don't think you are. I think if you could bear to admit it you might be ashamed, but you can't even do that. You're scared. Terrified. Of so much, of life, undeniably of love.

And we don't talk about it, men don't. Women think we gather in our hovels and drool and sneer and compare trading cards of our past conquests. Most of us are just so goddamn scared of getting it wrong. All that posturing is solely to convince the world that we have some fucking clue of what anything is.

MILT: I'm not scared. Okay? You don't know a goddamn thing.

AL: Sure. Yah, I'm—I probably don't. You're right.

   Beat.

MILT: When I was a kid, I used to get into fights. All the time, every day. After school, I'd take a shortcut home through the Irish neighbourhood—the working-class neighbourhood—and it wouldn't take long for one of those boys to want to teach me a lesson. I had middle-class blood, and they wanted to spill it. And I let them. Maybe as an act of political activism, but probably not. If I was out somewhere and nobody wanted to beat me up, I made 'em. I'd go find the biggest kid I could, tap him on the shoulder, and then whack him one. Some feeble punch is all it would take, and all I could honestly muster. Then they'd be on me, punching and kicking until I went down, and even after I was down, until someone pulled them off. Next day, I'd do it all over again.

Never won a fight in my life. Honestly never really tried. Wasn't about that.

Getting hit . . . it was the only way . . .

> *He trails off, not really knowing what to say or how to say it.*

I had a sister, a younger sister, and . . . when she was feeling scared or lonely or . . . not even a reason . . . I'd see her go to my folks, or anyone—her friends, school friends—she'd go and she'd . . . she'd ask 'em for a hug. She'd tug on a hem or a sleeve, and then she'd just open her arms real wide and close her eyes and wait for it. Imagine that. She'd get swept up in someone's arms and squeezed tight, then they'd set her down, rub her back or smooth her hair out . . . send her on her way. Imagine that.

> *Beat. He twists the end off a cigar stub and lights it.*

No one could figure out why I kept getting into fights I had no intention of winning.

I'm telling you, Al. Nobody even asked.

> *He goes quiet. That's enough for now.*

> AL *nods. He wants more than anything in the world to hug his friend. He wants to gather* MILT *Acorn in*

his arms and squeeze him tight, then rub his back
or smooth his hair out. He wants to tell him that he
understands. That he, too, got into fights he knew he
would lose, just to get hit. He wants to tell him that
he's not alone and he's not a freak and everything's
going to be okay. He wants to tell MILT *that he loves*
him and that he is a king. So AL *lights a cigarette.*
And he doesn't say or do any of those things. He
simply doesn't know how. None of us do.

AL: This should be enough.

> AL *takes an armload of twisted newspapers outside*
> *and puts them in the hole. He throws his lit cigarette*
> *in after them, then rushes back inside and closes*
> *the door.*

Cover your ears, soldier.

> MILT *is frozen. He just stares at* AL *and the closed door,*
> *and the knowledge of an explosive about to detonate*
> *creates a short circuit in his brain.*

Cover your ears, Milt!

Milt!

Goddammit.

> AL *rushes to* MILT, *kneels beside him and covers the*
> *other man's ears for him.* MILT *doesn't move. He just*
> *closes his eyes.*

The dynamite goes off with a resounding crack. A few small stones and dirt hit the walls of the A-frame. MILT's *body jerks up like he's been hit by lightning. His eyes open, but they are panicked and unseeing. He tries to run, to get away, but* AL *holds him down. He wraps his arms around* MILT's *body as it tries to escape what it thinks must be war.*

Hey! Hey.

Shh.

Hey. It's okay. It's okay.

You're okay.

MILT *eventually stops fighting. There are tears in his eyes. His breathing is laboured and short. They lie on the floor like this, a straight-jacket embrace.* MILT *seeing nothing,* AL *finally seeing everything.*

"If birds look into the window odd beings
look back and birds must stay birds.
If dogs gaze upwards at yellow oblongs
of warmth, bark for admittance
to hot caves high above the street,
among the things with queer fur,
the dogs are turned to dogs, and longing
wags its tail and returns invisible.

Clouds must be clouds always, even if
they've not decided what to be at all,
and trees trees, stones stones, unnoticed,
the magic power of anything is gone.
But sometimes when the moonlight disappears,
with you in bed and nodding half awake,
I have not known exactly who you were,
and choked and could not speak your name . . . ""*

> MILT *finally calms down. He just sort of slumps for-*
> *ward, and* AL *releases him. They stay there, on the*
> *floor, swaying in time with the cabin walls as they*
> *bow in the wind.*

---

* Al Purdy, "Whoever You Are," in *The Crafte So Long to Lerne* (Toronto: Ryerson Press, 1959), 19.

scene five: the last seized soul

*Some time later. There is now electricity in the A-frame.
The hydro pole can be seen outside the front window,
and electric lamps illuminate the interior. The walls
inside the construction area have been completed and
are in the process of being insulated. A mix of fibreglass
batts and crumpled-up newspaper are shoved into the
wall slats.* MILT *is angrily and systematically pulling
newspaper back out of the slats, opening them and
stuffing them back in.* AL *is reading.*

MILT: I can't believe you. What do I always say?

AL: You ask that as though there's only one answer.

MILT: "Save me the crossword." I always say to "save me the crossword." And what do you do? Stuff it in the wall. Don't even know
where.

AL: I'm reasonably sure it's that wall, I told you.

> MILT *gestures theatrically at all the goddamn paper in
> the wall.* AL *shrugs.*

It's not as if you really *do* the crossword, anyway.

MILT: G'wan, of course I do the crossword.

AL: Last week you wrote in *one* answer.

MILT: Those clues were indecipherable. You'd need to be Alan Turing to solve it. I oughta write them a letter. At least I got one answer. I'll bet you most people didn't even get that far.

AL: It was wrong.

MILT: How the hell do you know it was wrong?

AL: Sixteen down, the clue was "diagonally across from."

MILT: Yah. "Kitty-corner."

AL: Nope. Close. But wrong.

MILT: It fit, didn't it?

AL: Sure, it fit, but the sixteen across clue was "boorish."

MILT: Yah, and "Purdy" didn't fit.

AL: It's "coarse."

MILT: Do you know how crosswords work? "Coarse" doesn't start with "K," so it can't be "coarse."

AL: Unless . . .

MILT: "Kitty-corner" isn't wrong! "Diagonally across from" is *kitty-corner* from. The post office is kitty-corner from Grossman's Bar, the flower shop is kitty-corner from my barber—

AL: You go to a barber?

MILT: My foot is kitty-corner to your ass, but that might well change.

AL: It's "catty." "Catty-corner."

MILT: That's the dumbest thing you've ever said.

AL: We all *say* kitty-corner now, but it's not right. It's *catty*-corner.

MILT: Says who?

AL: It started with the English calling the four card in a deck "the *quatre* card," from the French. Didn't take long for that to turn from *quatre* to "cater," because the English are assholes. The four side of a die was called the "cater side" or "cater square" because of how the dots are laid out. That turned into cater-cornered, then catty-cornered, alliteration being the endgame of all language. So while we *say* kitty-corner, that's just an abomination of a prior abomination, et cetera et cetera.

    Beat.

MILT: Why don't we just say "across the street"?

AL: I don't really give a fuck, Milt.

He goes back to reading. MILT *stews for a bit.*

MILT: You always gotta show off.

AL: I'm not showing off.

MILT: You could've just said it was wrong. You didn't have to etymologize the whole goddamn crossword.

AL: I thought it was kind of interesting.

MILT: You've got this *tone* to you, you know that?

AL: What *tone?*

MILT: A *know-it-all* tone. I'll bet Eurithe hears it. I'll bet it drives her up the wall.

AL: I wouldn't be surprised. It's a long list of things that does.

Beat. He closes the book.

What's the problem, Milt?

MILT: What are you talking about?

AL: You've been caterwauling all goddamn night about everything from the insulation to the creak of the floorboards—

MILT: You used the wrong kind of wood!

AL: —I can't get two pages into this book without being hit by collateral damage from Hurricane Acorn. Can we skip to the end where you tell me what the problem is so you can feel better and I can read in some goddamn peace?

> MILT *takes out the newsletter from his pocket and tosses it to* AL.

MILT: I keep thinking about this.

AL: The conference?

MILT: It starts tomorrow. I'm getting restless here.

AL: Go, then.

MILT: I *can't.*

> MILT *lights a cigar and puffs on it stressfully.*

I don't have any good clothes.

AL: You can borrow something of mine.

MILT: I'd look like a goddamn Mormon.

AL: So we'll go down to the Sally Ann and get you something non-denominational.

MILT: *(dismissive)* It's fine.

AL: They've got one in Belleville, we can—

MILT: I don't have the money, Al. Unless they started trading poems for clothes.

> AL *nods his understanding. They sit in silence for a while.*

AL: It don't matter a damn. All poets are poor.

> *Silence.*

You think you'll be out of place?

MILT: Have you ever known me to fit in?

AL: If there was ever a time you would . . . it might be this.

> MILT *wrings his hands.*

MILT: I don't know.

> *Beat.*

AL: I told you about the taxi business. It going under and everything.

> MILT *nods.*

I told you about being up on that hill with the last unseized car, sending it into the lake. I didn't mention the very long time I sat inside the car, intending—maybe—to go over with it.

> AL *lights a cigarette. He draws on it, thoughtfully.*

I pictured myself doing it. In my imagination, it was poetic: the last unseized car, the last unseized soul. I played that scene over and over again, until I found the will to go on. I made it to Toronto, which—really—is only marginally better than dying.

I've killed myself a hundred times in my head.

Beat.

I think your politic is like that. Your deference to some Marxist rule about where you fit and where you don't. The doors you're allowed to walk through. Your obdurate belief in material limitations . . . it's a great excuse for not going through the doors you're terrified to open. It makes you a good Marxist and not a fucking chicken like the rest of us.

We both create fictions to skip over the parts of us that are frightened. The parts of us that are the most human.

MILT *growls.*

MILT: Even if you're right. Which you're *not.* I still don't have any good clothes.

AL: We can fashion you some out of newspaper.

AL *looks around.*

We seem to have used it for everything else.

MILT *shakes his head.*

72

MILT: I don't know.

AL: You *belong* there.

MILT: I barely belong *here.*

AL: Have some confidence.

MILT: Confidence? Confidence is for children. We don't deal in confidence—we live in the world. In the world, we know our strengths and our limitations, that is not a *fiction.* Idealism is fiction. Fatalism is fiction. Confidence is just bluster with makeup on. Confidence is the consolation prize of the untalented.

AL: Fine, don't go, then. I'm arguing with you like it matters to me.

> AL *crumples up the newsletter and pitches it into the stove.* MILT *dives for it.*

MILT: The hell are you doing?

> MILT *reaches into the stove and pulls the newsletter back out. It's a little bit on fire, but he stamps it out and smooths it back into legible condition.*

AL: It's settled then. I'll drive you as far as the highway. You can hitch from there.

> MILT *starts to protest.*

You don't plunge your hand into the inferno for unimportant things, Milt.

"They yearn for what they fear for."*

    MILT *silently acquiesces.*

I'll take you now, should give you time enough to find a ride that'll get you there by morning.

MILT: *(almost sheepishly)* Should I bring some copies of *In Love and Anger?*

AL: I thought you wanted them to take you seriously.

MILT: Go fuck yourself.

    AL *laughs.*

When I get back we're fixing those floorboards.

AL: Sure. Pack your things. I've got to see a man about a euphemism.

    AL *gets up. He notices a stray newspaper page under his seat. He examines it, then hands it to* MILT.

Will you look at that. I guess I did save it for you.

---

*   Dante Alighieri, *The Inferno,* Canto III.

He exits to the outhouse. MILT *grabs a pen and sits at the table to start the crossword. He taps it a few times against the desk, thinking. Suddenly, he's struck by a poem. He grabs a sheet of stationery and writes.*

MILT: When you look into your golden beer
and talk about suicide, Al,
I can't help dreaming laments,
obituaries, and how craftily
I'd cull my quotations
of you; half martyr
to this dusty tasting time
and half damned decadent

Like a green lignum vitae tree,
a nuisance on the lawn,
dead you'd carve into strong shapes,
living you're a problem.*

He props the poem up on the desk for AL *to find later. The action of this thrills him more than anything, the way leaving secret notes for your best friend will do.* AL *re-enters, swinging his car keys around his index finger like a gunslinger.*

AL: Now or never, Acorn.

MILT grabs a handful of cigars from a box by the table.

That's all you're bringing?

---

*   Milton Acorn, "Problem," *Moment* 1 (1961).

MILT: It's all I've got.

AL: Not even a fresh pair of socks? Underwear?

MILT: Bourgeois luxuries.

AL: Jesus Christ.

> AL *grabs a can of Glade air freshener and sprays* MILT *down. He coughs and sputters through it.* AL *pulls out the waistband of* MILT's *pants and sprays his delicates.*

Now you smell like fresh mountain air.

MILT: My eyes are burning.

AL: That's just gratitude. Take the can. Get in the car.

> *They walk out, shutting the door behind them.*

scene six: measure twice

The middle of the night. All is quiet and peaceful in the A-frame. And cold. AL *wakes up, shivering, and crosses to stoke the fire in the stove. While he's there, he decides to have a glass of wild grape wine. As he walks across the room, a floorboard creaks. He stops. He puts weight on it again, and it creaks louder. He tests it out a bit more, finally jumping up and down lightly on it.*

AL: It's fine.

Just then, the floorboard cracks, and his foot falls through. He swears loudly. He gently pulls his foot back up out of the floor and examines the hole.

Goddammit.

He's never gonna shut up about this.

Goddammit.

He walks into the construction area and turns on the utility lamp. It glows from off. He returns with a measuring tape. He measures the hole, grumbling to

*himself. He goes back to the construction area and
the sound of sawing ensues for a few moments. He
comes back on with a hole-sized piece of wood and a
hammer with some nails.*

*He gets on the floor and places the wood down. It just
sits on top of the hole. He tries forcing it, bringing it
down harder and harder, clapping it on the floor.*

Fuck.

*He goes off and returns with sandpaper. He starts
sanding the wood furiously.*

Piece of shit fucking wood.

He has a conversation with an imaginary MILT.

MILT: Measure twice, cut once, Al.

AL: I know, Milt, I know.

MILT: Should've used better wood, Al.

AL: Yah, yah, you're right, Milt.

MILT: You're sanding that wood too much, Al.

AL: Goddammit, Milt, get out of my head. I know how to sand a
piece of fucking wood.

AL *shakes his head to clear his friend out of it.*

I can build things, too, y'know. I'm not completely useless. I can fix a floor. Just a stupid floor, it's not rocket science.

> *He finishes sanding and blows on the wood. A small cloud of sawdust hangs in the air before gusting out one of the many drafty cracks in the foundation.*

> *Moment of truth.* AL *places the wood over the hole and drops it in place. It falls clear through, into the hole and out of sight.*

Oh for *crying out loud.*

> *He reaches into the hole to grab the errant wood. He tries to pull it back up, but it—somehow—gets stuck. He tries many times and can't manage to pull it out. He drops it back in the hole.*

Fuck's sake.

> *He breathes deeply. He has another swig of wine. He lights a cigarette.*

> *He gets the measuring tape out again and measures the hole. As he is about to get up, he makes an extra and obvious effort to measure the hole twice.*

Measuring *twice*, oh spirit of carpentry. Happy now?

> *He checks the tape, then goes back to the construction area. More sawing. He comes back in with another plank of wood.*

I swear to Christ I don't know how Eurithe did this by herself.

> *He measures the hole again. He measures the wood in his hand.*

Hah! Perfect. See that?

> *He holds the wood up so the gods can see. Then he drops it into the hole. It is, again, too big.*

No. No no no no no . . .

> *He slams it onto the floor again and again. Still won't fit.*

Fucking A-frame.

> *He yells into the hole.*

You're conspiring against me!

> *He grabs the wood, breaks it across his knee, and throws the pieces into the stove. With spite and vengeance in his heart, he throws the measuring tape, the hammer, and the nails in after it. He slams the stove door.*

> *He looks at the hole, steaming mad. He goes to the construction area and comes back with sheets of newspaper in both hands, a crazed look in his eyes. He starts stuffing the newspaper into the hole, but it just sort of disappears inside. So he takes a big sheet of*

newspaper, covers the hole with it. He grabs a staple gun from the construction area and staples the newspaper all around the hole. He stands up, sweating, admiring his work. It looks terrible.

AL looks around for something to make things better. His eyes land on the armchair where he likes to sit and read books. He drags the chair to one side and pulls up the rug, sliding it all over to cover the hole. He puts the chair on the rug, directly overtop the hole.

There.

He gives the armchair a little nudge with his foot. Nothing falls through the floor. He nods in satisfaction.

Wasn't that hard.

A satisfied AL Purdy goes back to sleep.

scene seven: shout

A couple of days later. AL *is touching up the back-door-frame casing. He is using a hammer head to drive in nails, as the handle burned to ash in the stove the other night.*

The front door opens. MILT *hangs in the doorway like a spectre.* AL *looks up.*

AL: Milt?

MILT doesn't answer. He's been outside a while, trying to gather the wherewithal to come in. He has deflated a bit. His shoulders are sunk a bit lower, his eyes fixed to the ground.

Milt? Come in, what are you doing?

MILT steps in and closes the door. He haunts the foyer, unsure what to do. AL *stops what he's doing and goes to meet him. They both stand in the main room, neither one really approaching the other.*

You okay?

MILT nods.

How was the conference?

MILT: Fine. Fine.

Beat.

How are things here?

AL: Um. Good. Fine. Yah.

(genuinely concerned) You sure you're okay?

MILT: Sure. Yah.

AL: And the conference went well?

MILT: Hm? Oh, yah. Great.

Beat.

You move the chair?

AL: What? Oh. Yah, I just . . . I like it better here.

MILT: S'in the middle of the room.

AL: It's not in the *middle* of the room. That's a touch hyperbolic.

MILT: Why would you put an armchair in the middle of the room?

AL: I like it better there. More natural light.

MILT: It was beside a window before.

AL: That window is south-facing, it only got *indirect* light.

> MILT *makes a face. He walks closer and studies* AL's *face. He walks around the chair. He bounces up and down a bit on the balls of his feet.*

MILT: The floorboards gave out and you moved the chair over the hole, didn't you?

> *Beat.*

AL: I also burned the hammer.

MILT: What?

AL: In the stove.

MILT: Why the hell would you do something like that?!

AL: It made me upset.

MILT: Jesus Christ, I go away for *two days* and everything falls apart.

> *Beat.*

Well, give me a hand.

They move the chair and rug off the hole. The news-
paper patch job is revealed. MILT *howls with laughter.*
He stops when he sees the embarrassment on AL's *face.*

Valiant effort, Al.

Pass me the thing.

AL *hands him the hammer head and* MILT *tears the news-*
paper away. He reaches under and pulls out the stray
board that fell through. He uses it to quickly measure
the hole, then takes it into the construction area and
saws out a new board. The speed and ease with which
he works is impressive. When he's not obsessing over the
task, one can see plainly he's had carpentry experience.
He moves like it's second nature, placing the new board
and tapping nails in to secure it. He works quietly, not
grumbling or complaining, deep in a sort of meditative
contemplation that belies the deep self-loathing inside.
He quickly sands the surface all while AL *watches in envy*
and awe. He finishes and scrutinizes the work.

It'll do for now.

They move the rug and chair back to where they ought
to live, and MILT *lights a cigar.*

Y'know it's true what they say about working with your hands.
The satisfaction you feel. You don't get that with poems. Maybe
you do, I don't know. But not me. The poem always feels unfin-
ished, even when it is.

Beat.

I'm good at this. Building things. I shouldn't have given it up so easy; trading couplings for couplets. It was impetuous. It was foolish.

I have a hardness in me that is ill-suited for poems. Men like me, we become tradesmen. Solid work, tangible . . . of the earth. The labour can be arduous . . . tedious and gruelling. But look at me. I'm built like this for a reason. You don't put a mule in a race among thoroughbreds.

Beat.

AL: *(carefully)* What did they do to you?

MILT *laughs softly.*

MILT: Nothing. They didn't do anything. This isn't them talking. It's me.

AL: Well, I don't much like what it is you're saying.

MILT: Well, it's not yours to like, is it.

Beat.

It's my darkness, Al. I'll do with it what I please.

Now, you've got a bad angle on the header, there. You need to straighten that out or it'll be trouble. I can get started on it—

He walks toward the back door, but AL *gets in his way.*

C'mon, Al.

AL: So you're just giving up? To hell with it all?

MILT: I'm just trying to fix the header.

He tries to get by, but AL *stands in the way again.*

AL: Quit being a baby, Milt. This isn't you.

MILT: *(snapping)* What do you know about it? What makes you the authority? I oughta crack you one for filling my head with fucking nonsense. "Have some confidence." What a load of shit you've been feeding me. Not that you believed it, anyway. You were just lonely in Neverland. Well tell it to the other Lost Boys, I've had it.

AL: So now you're making shit metaphors on purpose?

MILT: I'm fixing the fucking header because that's what I'm *for*, Al.

> MILT *tries to push past him, but* AL *still blocks his way.*
> MILT *growls.*

Get out of my goddamn way.

> AL *plants his hands square on* MILT's *chest and pushes*
> *him with some force.* MILT *is shocked and stumbles*
> *backward.*

AL: What the hell's the matter with you? Someone take your lunch money? Did they call you names? What happened?

MILT: Nothing happened! Quit pushing me!

AL *keeps pushing him around.*

AL: You know better than to listen to them! They rule with baseless authority, on empty merit. They're referees in a game they don't even know how to play. So, what? They didn't like your poems? Good. Fuck 'em. They'll write ten pages dissecting our usage of inter-rhyme and affect nothing. They don't decide our worth.

MILT: That's exactly what I said to *you*, and you said I was creating an elitist class!

AL: Well obviously I'm full of shit, Milt. I don't know what to tell you.

AL *gives* MILT *one final shove, then backs off and lights a cigarette.*

MILT: It's got nothing to do with that, anyway.

AL: Then what's it got to do with?

MILT: Forget it.

AL: Milton James Rhode Acorn. You will tell me what happened at that goddamn conference or I will tell everyone that you went to see *South Pacific* at the theatre *by yourself* on *three* separate occasions.

Beat.

MILT: I told you that in confidence.

AL: And you hum the tune to "Cockeyed Optimist" in your sleep.

MILT: You wouldn't dare, you right bastard.

AL: Try me.

   MILT stews. AL smokes. Time passes.

MILT: I didn't go.

   Beat.

AL: What?

MILT: I didn't go to the conference.

AL: Then where the hell have you been?

MILT: No, I *went* . . . I *physically* went . . .

   Deep breath.

It took a while after you dropped me in Belleville, but I finally
hitched with a trucker headed to Ottawa. He dropped me in
Kingston around seven a.m., and I hiked over to the campus.
Around nine, people started filtering in. By ten the place was lousy
with poets. Academics, too, all of them wearing some pullover

emblazoned with their college crest like it was a competition for who could look more like they deserved a punch in the face.

And there I was, a looming tree in the viney jungle of rhymers and reasoners. They snaked around me, filling their Styrofoam coffee cups and picking little Danishes off communal plates. Calling out to colleagues and friends across the hall, zipping off to some lecture or reading that was starting soon.

The poets were glad-handing and signing books in the middle of passing conversations. Robert Finch showed up. He was a big deal. The two Watsons—James and Wilfred. Ford. Reaney. Seemed like everyone there had a GG.

AL: They just give that thing away to anybody.

MILT: A woman who worked at the conference came up to me, asked if I was registered. I guess she was supposed to give me a name tag and got tired of staring at me staring at everyone else. She looked at me—sweetly, mind you, everything in Kingston is done sweetly—and she asked me my name.

    Beat.

I looked around at Reaney and Finch . . . they didn't have name tags. They didn't need them. People *know* who they are, and if they don't, they tap their neighbour and ask, "Hey, who's the guy getting all the attention?" Their neighbour will say, "Oh, well that's Robert Finch, don't you know. He wrote a collection of poems called *Poems* and they gave him the fucking GG for it."

    Beat.

I thought maybe Layton would come, show up at the last minute.
Even that asshole Dudek, I'd have settled for fucking Dudek.
They'd see me from across the lobby, call out my name, all con-
genial. We'd share tiny Danishes and laugh our asses off about
some fucking thing. But that didn't happen.

I also couldn't pay the registration fee, which, I guess if you're
someone like James Reaney you don't have to pay, but for two-bit
hacks like Milton Acorn it's twelve bucks, including a room at
the Holiday Inn. Now, it'll come as no surprise to you that I don't
have twelve bucks, so I found a nice bench in the park to sleep
on overnight.

> *Beat. He's embarrassed, but keeps going.*

They all . . . they looked right through me, Al. Not a single
person knew my name or my poems. I'm pretty sure they thought
I was the janitor after a while, judging by how many people com-
plained to me about the state of the men's john.

And the thing is . . .

> *He takes a puff of his cigar and paces around a bit.*

I'm a better poet than they are! I know it's not Canadian to say,
but fuck it, Al, it's true. I'm a better goddamn poet than half of
those guys. They write quiet little iambics about tufted titmice
meant to be read softly over glasses of sherry at the A & L club.
They don't know the first goddamn thing about *life*. They write
about darkness as the absence of light, not a thing which — when
wrestled with — fights back. Tries to destroy you. They write
about love as if it wasn't freshly painted pain. They *want*, sure,

everybody *wants*, but they do not *ache* the way my heart *aches*, Al. And they *cannot* build a goddamn *house*!

But they've got a GG and I've just got—

> *He fishes copies of* In Love and Anger *out of his coat pocket and throws them on the floor.*

—three *self-published* chapbooks with fucking *typos*.

> *Beat.* MILT *is exhausted. He eases himself down into the armchair.* AL *smokes, thoughtfully. They are quiet for a time.*

AL: You idiot.

> MILT *starts to protest.*

No, I get it. Okay? I *get* it. I understand. But you're still an idiot.

Twenty some odd years ago, T.S. Eliot's mag *The Criterion* was going to publish something by one of his two young proteges. It would be either Stephen Spender or W.H. Auden. Unable to decide which, he took them both out to lunch. Auden got there first, and by the time Spender showed up, the other two were in deep conversation. Finally noticing he was there, Eliot turned and said, "I wanted to ask you both, as we are going to publish one of you, very simply . . . what is it you want to *do*?"

Spender looks Eliot dead in the eye—he'd been waiting for this day. He tells him, "I want to be a poet."

Eliot goes, "Well, I don't know how to go about doing *that*." And they just start laughing. Right in the guy's face. But Spender doesn't know what he's said wrong.

He looks at Auden, his old schoolmate, and he asks him, "Well, what did *you* say?"

And Auden tells him: "I said I wanted to write poems."

> *Beat.* MILT *growls.*

MILT: So you're saying, what? I'm Spender, you're Auden? Who's Eliot, Layton?

AL: That isn't what I'm saying, you insecure bag of cats. I'm saying to hell with recognition, to hell with book signings and bullshit awards. I'm saying the poem business isn't about the adoration of the public, it's about fucking *poems*.

> *Beat.*

MILT: Gwen was there.

AL: Gwen . . . MacEwen?

> MILT *nods.*

Did you talk to her? Did she see you?

> MILT *shakes his head.*

MILT: I hid behind a ficus tree.

She was talking with Robert Finch. He signed her copy of *Poems*. She was laughing and . . . he said something and she touched his arm. The way girls do. She touched my arm like that one time, after a reading.

AL: You didn't say anything to her?

MILT: What do I say? "Hi, when you met me you thought I was somebody, but now it's obvious I'm nobody."

AL: Well, I wouldn't say *that*, no.

MILT: A mule among thoroughbreds.

Beat. AL *sighs.*

AL: What are you going to do about it?

MILT: What can I? My circumstance is what it is. Only fools like Al Purdy think we can change that.

AL: "Since we are what we are, what shall we be
But what we are? We are, we have
Six feet and seventy years, to see
The light, and then release it for the grave.
We are not worlds, no, nor infinity,
We have no claims on stone, except to prove
In the invention of the city
Our hearts, our intellect, our love"*

---

* Stephen Spender, "Since we are what we are, what shall we be," *Poems of Dedication* (New York: Random House, 1947), 41.

MILT: Auden?

AL: Spender. Because we're all full of shit, Milt. Even you. *Especially* you.

> *Beat.*

So what's it going to be, Milt? You gonna write the poems that make the girl touch your arm? Or are you gonna hide behind a ficus the rest of your life?

> *Beat.* MILT's *heartbeat ticks away into the evening, ever quickening at the thought of Gwen, and faster at the prospect of losing her attention.*

What did you write?

MILT: Hm?

AL: While you were there. You write any poems?

MILT: What, while I was sleeping on the park bench? No, I didn't have the occasion to write any fucking poems. There were enough poets laureate around, I figured they'd take care of it.

AL: You're alone all evening with no booze, a pocketful of cigars, and a heart full of regret. You're telling me you didn't write a poem.

MILT: I didn't have any paper.

AL: You don't write with paper; you write with your heart.

MILT: Put that on a greeting card, please.

AL: What did you write out there in the cold Kingston air?

MILT: *Nothing.*

AL: There is something on your tongue. I can see it when you bark at me.

MILT: I didn't write any fucking poems.

> *Beat.* AL *stares at him.*

It's not done yet.

AL: Hit me.

MILT: I don't even know what it is, yet.

AL: Lay it on me.

MILT: It's not good enough.

AL: Show me what you got, you fucking carpenter!

> MILT *explodes.*

MILT: "I SHOUT LOVE!"

> *A breath.*

"I shout love in a blizzard's
scarf of curling cold,
for my heart's a furred sharp-toothed thing
that rushes out whimpering
when pain cries the sign writ on it.

I shout love into your pain
when skies crack and fall
like slivers of mirrors,
and rounded fingers, blued as a great rake,
pluck the balled yarn of your brain.

I shout love at petals peeled open
by stern nurse fusion-bomb sun,
terribly like an adhesive bandage,
for love and pain, love and pain
are companions in this age."*

> *A long beat.* MILT *is out of breath.* AL *is breathless.*
> *They stare at each other, like a bomb has just gone off*
> *between them.*

Should I write it down?

> AL *shakes his head.*

AL: No. No, you remember the good ones.

---

* Milton Acorn, "I Shout Love," in *I Shout Love and Other Poems* (Toronto: Aya Press, 1989), 23.

They are silent. The wind picks up and rattles the doors of the A-frame. The ice cracks in Roblin Lake. The two men wordlessly go back to the business of building a house. Everything is becoming something else. Everything is becoming greater than it is.

End of play.

acknowledgements

Special thanks to Ryan Hollyman, Philip Akin, Kevin Hanchard, and Carlos Gonzalez-Vio for your various turns as Al and Milt in workshop and production. Your generosity and feedback were instrumental in making this play what it is. My sincere thanks to Howard White and Eurithe Purdy for their blessings; Gypsy and TMJ for their encouragement; Joanna Yu, Michelle Ramsay, and Christopher Stanton for their gorgeous and influential production design (especially Joanna for her ad hoc construction and carpentry advice); Matt McGeachy for his perspicacity, insight, and willingness to follow me down any rabbit hole I wander into; and to Nina Lee Aquino for being the best partner-in-art a guy could ask for.

Sue Zhou has shared and enabled my obsession with poetry over the last decade. She enables me in most things, if I'm honest, but I feel like we're the artists and people we are because we can always count on each other for blind, uncompromising support. Even when we're wrong. Especially when we're wrong.

Vienna Hehir had to hear me drone on about poetry, reading her snippets of poems and interviews, and put up with an ever-growing stack of poetry books in our cramped little apartment during two years of lockdown. I was able to fully appreciate the depth of the love Al had for Eurithe, the love of his life, only because I had the love of mine with me.

David Yee is a mixed-race (half Chinese, half Scottish) playwright and actor born and raised in Toronto. He is the co-founding artistic director of fu-GEN Theatre Company, Canada's premiere professional Asian Canadian theatre company. A Dora Mavor Moore Award–nominated actor and playwright, his work has been produced internationally and at home. He is a two-time Governor General's Literary Award nominee for his plays *lady in the red dress* and *carried away on the crest of a wave*, which won the award in 2015 along with the Carol Bolt Award in 2013. He has worked extensively in the Asian Canadian community as an artist and an advocate. outlawpoet.ca